Dance with Broken Language

Poems for Spiritual Seeker

Dance with Broken Language

Poems for Spiritual Seeker

By Young Jun Kim

Order this book online at www.trafford.com
or email orders@trafford.com

Most Trafford titles are also available at major online book retailers.

© Copyright 2011 Young Jun Kim.
All rights reserved. No part of this publication may be reproduced, stored in a retrieval
system, or transmitted, in any form or by any means, electronic, mechanical, photocopying,
recording, or otherwise, without the written prior permission of the author.

Printed in the United States of America.

ISBN: 978-1-4269-6323-0 (sc)
ISBN: 978-1-4269-6325-4 (hc)
ISBN: 978-1-4269-6324-7 (e)

Library of Congress Control Number: 2011904837

Trafford rev. 04/07/2011

 www.trafford.com

North America & international
toll-free: 1 888 232 4444 (USA & Canada)
phone: 250 383 6864 ♦ fax: 812 355 4082

To my mother and father, Ae Sook Park and Doo Pyo Kim.
To Erskine Theological Seminary, GCU, and MeSun Hospice.

"What is man that you are mindful of him, the son of man that you care for him?"
— Psalms 8:4

Table of Contents

Preface

Writing poems makes me feel arrogant enough; writing them without the knowledge of language makes me feel guilty. But I wanted to record traces of my life to give my children, as a father, and my wife, as a husband. To send thoughts to a stranger's mind is a kind of vocational job, I think. Some poems send an empty mind, and some poems are expressed with spiritual thirst. Some poems are sending a hidden, divine being—my Lord—and some send struggles about my immigrant ministry. And also I tried to send my emptiness as a wandering stranger who is seeking a spiritual answer from inner voices.

I hope and pray my small foot traces will offer someone a chance to see my Lord, and I want to meet some reader through my poems in the future.

The writer wrote this book's title as *Dance with Broken Language*. What does it mean, *Dance with Broken Language*? It might be from my guilty feeling about my inability to express my inner mind in English. So I wanted to write, through poetry, a book of broken language—chaotic yet expressive, like the wind. The language is descriptive, but my expressions may be enigmatic. Please understand this writer as a naive guy who likes to express his emotions even without knowing language.

Thanks to Trafford; my wife, Mee Sook Song Kim; and four children, Lee-Lye Kim, Ee Sl Kim, Isaac Kim, and Isaiah Kim.

A Moment of Humiliation

There are uncountable humiliations in our lives

The moment is always timeless

Most existing

With emptiness

With vanity

With contradiction

With wrestling

Me and God

And then,

A moment of understanding

No Man's Land

There is a no man's land.

It is not the land of Verdun, France.

It is my backyard.

Tangling roots, burning sun, and heated soil refuse humans approaching.

But only one person, they accept.

Who?

The man who knows how to be human,

and who knows the essence of relationship

with God.

A Cup of Coffee

A cup of coffee

Freedom of pretending

Form of nobility

Emptiness

Remaining of warm

For a second

Empty chair

Tranquil Highway

Man leaves his traces

Each trace has its story

stories of desire, envy, love, regret, anger, joy, stupid, faith, struggle, sins ...

Some way remains with trash highway

Some way remains with tranquil highway

Life never guarantees the tranquil highway

So we pray

A Present of First Snow

A heavy, snowy day

It is a lucky day

due to unexpected resting

It is a present from heaven

to be alone with rest

A strange time

having been used to being busy with something

but always with an empty hand

Today I find full of fruits

without busyness

even alone in my home

all day long

due to a heavy snow

A heavenly present

I have met with a strange guest

Me

Under the Cultural Tolerance

The Korean Peninsula, the American continent, and the Deep South:

judgment, presupposition, and ignorance.

But I would like to express

the country of opportunity,

the country of rationalism,

the country of patriotism—

all are attractive, so I am still here.

Under the cultural tolerance, I was accepted in here.

If I am saying that I am experiencing cultural tolerance,

will be there someone who glares at me?

The country that accepts a stranger,

the country that suggests a nest to a stranger …

I cannot stop praying for this country.

Due to that, I am a stranger.

Due to that, my generation will flourish here

and they will be a part of American history

under the cultural tolerance.

Next Generation

Sometimes I imagine what my descendants will be.

Will they be professors, ministers, missionaries, soldiers, lawyers, politicians, medical doctors, engineers, entertainers, artists, pilots, merchants, and so on?

What I worry about is their evaluation of me.

Will I be a great forefather, like Abraham, or shameful, like Lot?

Life is like a seedling.

How can I be a good soil for those seeds?

In this question, I feel I am a loser to my sons.

I have guilty feelings due to not being a good father.

Someday I would like to disappear from my sons,

because I don't want to be a burden to them.

My prayer is to disappear like Moses, with good health,

to somewhere like Mount Nebo.

There, I will repent to God.

When a Daughter Doesn't Come Home

When a daughter doesn't come home

I cannot sleep

Even I don't have any expectation of a daughter

due to too much disappointment

But because I am a father

I cannot sleep, but only pray

Is this the mystery of fatherhood? Or the love of fatherhood?

Anyhow, I cannot sleep

Trap

Life is a trap

Sometimes, I wonder where I stand in the Deep South

Now, I am losing where I have stood

Just like a stranger who is running into a trap

Sometimes I question God

Why did my Lord allow the trap into my life?

Why did you bring me into this huge land I never know?

I know nobody knows their destination

just running into a trap

but a meaningful trap

Sandwich

Life is sandwiched between conflict, man and man

Life is sandwiched between struggle, me and me

Life is sandwiched between zeal, me and God

One Shoe

When I lost my one shoe on the sand of the Han River

my father tried to find that shoe

because we were poor

When my father left our home

"Papa, don't go," I said

Shame and shame

Sorry and sorry

Guilty feeling, still now

Due to one shoe reflecting my father's love

If I could pay the love to my father

I would live without shoes forever

When I Can't Sleep

When I can't sleep, I try to stand on the rock

but I can't stand on there, I only stand on air

Try and try

Fail and fail

Why?
.
.
.

Do I stand in abyss?

When I can't sleep, I journey alone, like a wandering jellyfish

The highest moment of existing

due to a time to be foolish

Dance with Death

Whenever I meet a person who is dying,

I feel mountainous guilt

grow from my immaturity, a lack of knowledge of how to help those miserable people,

and also the barrier between present and eternity

Even I should be a man between death and life, but I am always full of life

A mystic distance exists between a person seizing to survive and a person seizing

to release his life; how can I measure that distance?

Would the distance be a contradiction?

Or a mystery?

The gap between present and eternity

Impossible dance with those people who are going to eternity

Just I feel my guilt rise
.
.
.

Simply praying for forgiveness and repentance

Death

Death is a way of eternal healing

Death is a way of realizing real love

Death is a way of releasing everything

Death is a way of grasping everything

Death is a way of journeying to mystery, to eternity

Death is a way of knowing human beings

Death is a way of recognizing the omnipotence of God

Death is a way of confirming the revelation of God

Reality and Illusion

Money is reality,

Right,

Nobody deny that,

Right,

Money is fake fantasies,

Right,

Reality is money,

Right,

Illusion is money,

Right,

Endless confusion

Clouds, Nobody Knows

Nobody knows how we are living here

Likewise, clouds go and stop

Nobody knows how we experience some struggle in some spot

Likewise, clouds go and stop

Nobody knows what the meaning of life is here

Likewise, clouds go and stop

But who knows who reins clouds?

Love Is Like a River

Love is like a river

because it flows without any word

Love is like a river

because it is patient

Love is like a river

because it is timeless

Love is like a river

because it creates a pebbles

Love is like a river

because it delivers the best sermon

A Stranger Somewhere in the Deep South

I am a stranger in the Deep South

I don't know how I came here

but I know I am a stranger

With warm eye contact, human communication with Southerners, even I wish

But barriers rise due to differences

I am a stranger

I understand barriers mean human sin

A common ground is universal, always

Here and there

Timeless, happening in human ground

River

River flows with space—less

It flows with time—less

No end,

but it ends in my mind

Presence of God

Sky is blue

Bird is singing

Wind is breezing

Presence of God is everywhere

Life Is Accidental

Life is accidental,

It causes a lot of agonies,

unwanted happenings in our lives

Is this universal?

God always teaches us the value of accidental happenings,

eschatology

Wake up wake up wake up

Where Is God?

God is in humans' scars

Because everybody has scars

Those scars each have a story and wisdom

When we open our minds, we can hear His voice through our scars

Isn't it a mystery?

Yes or no?

My prayer is to realize His destiny in my scars

I Shall Not Want

"I shall not want"

These words are most mysterious to me

Because I need money, health, knowledge, wisdom, leadership, a good character, safe places, good relationship skills, forgiveness, tolerance, love, the Holy Spirit, sanctification, and so on …

How can I confess "I shall not want"?

It is impossible

Yes, this is human existence

"I shall not want"

Yes, this is God's existence

"I shall not want"

Is this a gate to the recognition of human existence?

Yes

Is this a gate to the recognition of God's existence?

Yes

Dual gate

"I shall not want"

A gate to get heavenly rest

Dandelions in My Yard

Dandelions in my yard

Yellow flowers

Even you are charming and pretty

but you make me ashamed

Due to your beautiful flower in green

Dandelions in my yard

Yellow flowers

Even you are charming and lovely

I should get rid of you

because you make me ashamed

Why did you fly into my yard?

Didn't you know?

You are a sacrifice for my shame

Don't you know?

This land is humans' land

.

.

.

I am sorry

Bread

Someone was throwing away a bunch of breads

I hoped to inhibit that guy's behavior

with these words: "Can you give me that bread to feed my dog?"

But inside, my voice said, "Can you give me that bread to feed me and my kids?"

Was I experiencing the memory of hunger or the desire of possession?

Anyhow, I wanted to save that bread,

because bread cannot be trash

but it should be my dung

Endless Crying of Waves

Waves,

why are you crying?

Because you crossed over the Gulf coast?

You have taken such a long journey, but nobody recognizes your harsh life,

so you are crying.

I understand,

though harsh life is your reality, and you been through much,

nobody recognizes you,

so you are crying.

That's reality,

at the seashore,

at your last destination,

being broken and diminished,

so you are crying.

But your need is recognized

through your break and disappearance,

and you are creating healing to many.

When an Old Song Is Repeating

I didn't know why I sang an old song repeatedly.

The song was, "I love you, really love you."

Its rhythm was smooth and warm.

Even I tried to stop this song,

this secular song,

but I couldn't stop it.

I know

the power of nature—

was my inability to stop

due to

a tangling with sin?

To know me

is

always mysterious.

Breeze

Breeze is an unexpected friend who is touching my cheek.

Breeze is an unexpected presence of spirit who is whispering to my soul.

Breeze is an unexpected comforter who is healing my hurt.

To Be or Not to Be

There is a lot of "to be or not to be" in our lives.

When I purchase a one-dollar thing, it is sometimes a decision of "to be or not to be."

When I feel my self-esteem being ignored, it turns to "to be or not to be."

What a pitiful happening in my life the situation of "to be or not to be" is.

Due to my stupidity,

due to my sin,

due to my ignorance,

due to

due to

due to

A Portrait

Sometimes I want to visit the bench under a Platanus tree at the old elementary school.

To search my portrait of my young days,

to talk with myself,

to talk with the lover of mine in those young days.

What did I say?

What did I hear?

I want to ask the Platanus tree

what I said,

what I heard

A Feather

A feather at seashore,

a feather is dancing with wave.

But you should be in the sky,

so I am asking, where is your body?

Were you flying in the sky

with vision,

with hope,

with dream?

But now you remain only a feather.

I want to hear your story

of when you were flying high,

when you were vision, hope, and dream.

Whispering

Whispering to my L

with unceasing stories,

with an impossible conclusion for our future

Whispering, whispering, whispering

sad memories,

almost-forgotten memories

But the memories are dwelling in my nature,

inerasable memories,

still scars in my soul,

singing in my ears with whispering, whispering, whispering

A Song at the Café

Relaxing at the café,

A song I never heard,

Noisy sound,

A gap of generation?

Now and then?

Or,

A gap of location?

Here and there?

Same thing is a behavior of existence,

That is a universal sign,

Everyone expresses their inner voices,

Due to human being,

Due to emptiness of being,

Lonesome song

Memories

When I met my wife, she bought bananas for me,

because she had asked me, "Which fruit do you want to eat most in the world?"

It is a childish memory.

When I married her without any money,

she gave me money to marry.

It is a selfish memory.

When I saw her tearful eyes for me,

it is a lovely memory.

Childish memories,

selfish memories,

lovely memories.

But now I am creating

ugly memories,

but meaningful memories,

due to the tolerance of God.

Tear

Tear is a power to heal my mind

Tear is a needle to cure my soul

Tear is a friend to purity

Tear is a gate to spiritual recognition

Tear is eyes of heavenly knowledge

Tear is eyes without eyes

Tear is a merciful lip to dialogue with God

To Be a Stranger

To be a stranger

It is easy

Too easy to be a stranger

Without any effort

Without any agonizing

To be a stranger is too natural

Alienation is so familiar to us

Is life a kind of used to be a stranger?

I don't know

But who knows? Who loves a stranger?

Unexpected Happenings

Is science

for avoiding uncountable, unexpected happenings?

I don't know

but I know we have tried to get happiness

If we can avoid unexpected happenings

if we can foresee our future

we would avoid tremendous tragedy

but nobody knows the future

All we can do is see the hidden meaning in the unexpected happening

Reality always remains an interpretation

The Yard, My Old Lover

A long time ago, I had a scar

This scar sometimes led me to step into the yard of my old lover,

even though she left a long, long time ago

Still, I am stepping into the yard of my old lover,

even though I feel it shameful, due to my loving wife

But sometimes I am stepping into the yard

Why?

A part of my being has remained at the yard.

Even though almost thirty years have passed,

a part of my being is still there.

Is this a behavior of looking for me

or looking for her?

I don't know.

Is life like this, tangling with a part of mine?

A Shower of a Summer Day

To be like a shower of a summer day,

it is too hard

To be stubborn on a hot summer day,

it is too easy

Not only heat, but also humidity and dizziness

Those are so easy

Sometimes I ask myself,

"How can you be a cool man?"

I say "Only God can do."

Only God can do …

is this a hiding place of a believer's folly?

Toward 55

Life is giving up

Due to age

It is common sense to most men

Still, can I have energy like a young man?

Stupidity

There are tremendous questions like that

To be free is to know my reality

To be visionary,

that's wisdom

To be myself ,

that's the way of divine knowledge

Toward 55,

the age of knowing how to be nature,

the age of hungering to feel divine will

Toward 55

To Be Like an American

To be like an American,

a pretender

To be like an American,

diverse

To be like an American,

spoiled

To be like an American,

puritanical

To be like an American,

tolerant

To be like an American,

arrogant

Divine Time

Divine time is accidental time

Divine time is faithful time

Divine time is ordinary time

Divine time is sacrificing time

Divine time is crying time

Divine time is virtue time

Divine time is suffering time

Divine time is enigmatic time

Divine time is eschatological time

Homesickness

Homesickness is like

Running clouds,

Wind,

River,

Mountain,

Old village,

Old friends,

Father and mother,

Forgetting,

Old pictures,

Wrinkles,

Passed away …

Faith

Faith is timeless

Faith is cultureless

Faith is eyeless

Faith is earless

Faith is mouthless

Faith is religionless

Back and Forth

Back and forth at the court

Authoritative officers like near gods

Nobody knows where to go

At the court, everybody turns to county boys

Almost all people are black

in downtown Atlanta

and a few Asians

Each tries to avoid eye contact

Only back and forth

at the court of innocent people

Cumming, Where I Live

I never knew Cumming, Georgia.

"Cumming,"

does it mean welcoming everybody?

But this was a notorious place

due to segregation

not long ago.

But I am living here because of God's destination.

Whenever I think of my town,

I cannot stop meditating on God's sovereignty and people's tolerance.

A place of sunshine,

a welcoming town,

Cumming.

Alone in the church

The most pleasant time is being alone at the church,

because nobody hinders me

Writing, reading, scribing, sleeping, praying, imagining …

It is a most happy time

because I am an immigrant minister

Splendid America

American is a country like an invisible binding—

binding with money, legalism, barriers, and imagination

Mysteriously, people become a cultural slave to those bindings

Without money, nobody is guaranteed freedom

Without knowing the law, nobody is guaranteed comfort

Without becoming accustomed to culture, nobody is guaranteed freedom from barriers

Splendid nation

Tremendous people sought the kingdom of God, so they came to America

but homesick

desperately seeking eschatological hope

Critical Days

There are tremendous, critical days in our lives.

These days are harsh, and people want to avoid them.

Avoiding critical days is natural,

because nobody wants harsh suffering and pain,

but it can't be avoided

because the critical days always visit suddenly

The wisdom of life is welcoming those critical days

because it is divine time

A Night I Cannot Sleep

In a deep night, I would like to write a poem, due to hardly sleeping.

On a night I cannot sleep, I would like to call my friend in my mother's land.

"Hello!"

"What are you doing? Everything okay?"

With even those three communications, I would be satisfied,

because I want to confirm he is still my friend.

On a night I cannot sleep, I will do my prayer to communicate with my Lord,

because I want to confirm He is my friend who will take my soul.

On a night I cannot sleep, I want to rely on Him with my entire burden,

because I want to confirm the victory.

On a night I cannot sleep, I will be free from all yokes.

Mosquito Coil

Mosquito coil, I only need you on the summer night.

Mosquito coil, I only need you when I feel risk from mosquitoes.

Mosquito coil, you make me ashamed that I rely on you.

Mosquito, without any word, how much are you intimidating me?

Mosquito, how much should I learn from the power of silence?

A Long, Long Time Ago

A long, long time ago, I met one girl,

when I was a soldier,

at the age of twenty-three,

at the church near my army camp.

With the expectation to see her, I often visited that church,

but in my stupidity, I tried to distance myself from her,

because she was less educated.

From this stupidity, she might have scars on her heart.

Now, why do I have guilty feelings in my fifties?

Is this evidence of my maturity?

It's too late to say sorry after three decades.

How can I heal her hurt?

Only I can give forgiving prayer with weeping,

weeping for me.

Uncountable mistakes in my life

might make a pile bigger than Mount Cherokee.

If I Meet Young Myself

If I meet young myself,

what can I say to me?

"Hi! Kim, you are a naive guy!"

But I will soon realize that he doesn't have any ear to hear from me,

because of the phrase "a naive guy."

Full of himself,

full of myself—

still I am full of myself, I know.

But a difference between now and then is

I am getting to understand the meaning of "a naive guy."

What a long journey from head to heart is!

When I realize the phrase "a naive guy,"

I may understand the meaning of humanity.

Hopefully.

Isaac, Inner Dynamic Guy

Isaac, inner dynamic guy, I want to be like you

Isaac, inner dynamic guy, I want to have your obedience

Isaac, inner dynamic guy, I want to take my cross to deny me

Into the Fire

Into the Fire—have you heard of this movie title?

There were deaths of seventy-one students

in the Korean War.

We know we are debtors due to tremendous young deaths in the war

like those students' deaths.

To save their nation,

to save their family,

to save their lives,

they chose to abandon their lives.

Life is not a fight for how to live long;

it is a fight for how to live like a flame,

so I regret a living like amber.

To Be a Soulless Man

It is easy to be a soulless man.

When someone backbites me without any fault of mine,

that is a moment to be a soulless man.

When someone judges me without any reason,

that is a moment to be a soulless man.

When I make a mistake and hurt someone,

that is a moment also to be a soulless man.

How many times will I experience such a soulless situation?

Is life used to a soulless man?

Due to my stupidity?

Due to someone's stupidity?

Due to God's loving touch?

Cerements

Do I have cerements?

Yes, I have.

The cloth I wear now is cerements,

because I don't know a time to die.

All men are dressed in cerements,

but nobody knows that they are dressed in cerements.

That is folly.

Everybody is walking to death, day by day.

That is a most universal fact.

Do cerements symbolize life and death?

I don't know.

But the fact is, we are dressed in death.

So we are dancing with death every day.

It is a mystery of life.

Recognizing death is a way to become sage, peaceful, humble, eternal, and free.

The important thing is, death always creates an unfinished mission in our lives,

so nobody can avoid humility before death.

A person who recognizes that his dressing is his cerements is a holy sage.

Lord, give me the open eyes!

I Saw My Friend Dressed in Cerements

I saw my friend dressed in cerements the day he passed away.

In an exercise uniform, a blue sweater, and white pants,

on a windy day, he stood far from me, and his face was strangely pale.

I don't know why he was not smiling that day—

lonely, lonesome, solitarily alone on that day.

Did he know the day as his last day?

Is it natural for a human being to know his last day?

Due to spiritual being?

Due to subconscious?

Due to a being who recognizes death?

But nobody can avoid invading death, even if they recognize their deaths.

That we call destiny.

But there might be two kind of destiny:

the destiny with eschatological hope

or

the destiny toward ordinary death.

Tower of Babel

Sometimes, I am murmuring.

Why did people build the Tower of Babel?

Was it power of sin?

Tremendous burdens weigh on people's reality.

Likewise, organic sin,

power of omnipresence—

we call it a language barrier.

The Babel tower is Babel power:

bringing tyranny,

multiplying language barriers,

multiplying alienation,

creating stupidity,

and faking motion.

A tool of recognition, human's existence,

a contradictory situation,

frustration.

Babel tower, origin of all evil power,

even though I would like to call the Babel tower a bubble tower.

An Alien

Culture, language, skin color, and dominance

Often, I don't know where I am standing

A lot of barriers by arrogance

Why do people try to create barriers?

I know the power of sin

Arrogance, superficiality, and judgment

To aliens? Or to themselves?

Losing expectation

to Americanism

but gaining a divine hope

To Talk with People Who Are Passing Away

To talk with people who are passing away becomes my life journey—

a journey of guilt

due to my unskillful relationship, touch, communication, eye contact, body language,

and so on.

How can I wash away these guilty feelings?

Those people who are passing away know of my heart when I visit them,

tangling with business,

but their tolerance always accepts me with a smile.

When people admit to journeying toward death, they eagerly open their minds, without

any business.

This is a true way of living, a real way of being free, and a wise way of recognizing

the essences.

When a Person Has a Question about Death

When a person has a question about death,

they want my answer as their answer,

because none of them have experienced death.

So I would like to say,

most difficult business,

most burdening business,

most guilty business—

that's hospice business.

To be a friend to a dying person at the end of his journey of life

is a real incarnation.

Like an impossible mission

without understanding humanity, with guilty feelings,

this business is never understood.

The most difficult business is when the technician ages,

tremendous traps to care for the dying person,

contradictorily.

No Hope

Where is hope?

It is diminishing magic.

Hope is an attractive thing,

but grasping it is like an impossible business.

So, I remain a loser and a failure.

Someone whispers me with a revolving voice,

you are a loser and a failure.

Yes, yes, I know.

Knowing no hope,

too much easy business

to besiege with no hope—

that is a man's nature.

But without hope, how a man can live?

From the morning, I have looked for hope with all my strength.

Where is hope?

Hope is where

.

.

You.

To Be a Father

To be a father at the age of no authority

Means being a father like a feather

Relationship between human and human at the first stage

Relationship between human and machine at second stage

Relationship between human and enigmatic being

And relationship between human and a feather

But a meaningful feather, like a bridge for the next generation

To be a father is a most blessed job and privilege

Even being called a feather, I will never regret it

Salvation Is Secret

Salvation is secret

Nobody knows this secret except God

It is total grace

It is the perfect work of God

It starts from God's choosing behavior

Veiling plan by God

Revelation

Predestination

Eternal being

Timeless being

Who knows this secret?

When I Feel No Answer to My Prayer

I seize skepticism due to no answer to my prayer,

but I start to negotiate with my faith: "That's a natural thing."

As a length between death and life, the behavior of prayer has a mystical length

due to no answer.

How can I define a life?

Is it a fight with reality and skepticism?

A journey of frustration,

but only a way to God?

God Himself is the answer.

That's it.

Wind and Life

I often pray for a person who is going to the end of life

Even my mystical expression, "Wind!"

Those people give nodding at my word, "wind"

"Wind!"

The most appropriate expression as a life

Leaving no trace, diminishing, forgetting, and erasing tremendous stories, but nobody knows

what a life is!

But we believe heaven knows one's wind trail, trace, and footprint

It makes people be honest

Very mystical lesson

Journey and a Stranger

How many journeys did I have in my life?

One, two, three, four, or uncountable journeys?

I don't know,

but I feel they were tremendous journeys.

Each journey had several ways,

but choosing was like a dance with wind—

so mystical

due to my ignorance.

Nobody knows his or her future,

so universal truth:

in my fifties,

strangely, I am leaning toward the providence of God

and my desire to know about the divine knowledge.

Someday I will confirm His knowledge in heaven.

A Pebble Stone

A pebble stone

Rounding stone

A stone who knows being wind

A stone who knows being water

A stone who knows being hurt

A stone who knows being humble

A stone who knows being nature

Two Glasses Leaf

Two glasses leaf

It looks meaningless

Nobody considers it

Looks like a folly

Anonymous people

Being treated like two glasses leaf

To be ignoring

To be trashing

To be emptying

.

.

To be winning

To Be a Fool

To be a fool

It is a way to know happiness

To be a fool

It is a way to be free

To be a fool

It is a way to be peace

To be a fool

It is a way to be a sage

To be a fool

It is a way to be wisdom

To be a fool

It is a way to be divine

Language

Someone calls a language a house of being

But to me, it becomes a struggle of being

Because it requires culture, eye contact, love, and spirit

A language is a universal tool, but without love,

Without love

Without love

Who can make communication with this divine tool?

Soon after speaking out

Turn it to corruption

Is the best language silence, listening, and love?

Heavenly Languages

Heavenly languages

We can see the languages in nature

The sound of stream, brook, and river

The sound of wind, clouds, and rain

The sound of animals, bugs, and birds

Full of sound in the world

Even they never speak

But they are speaking with one language

So they know how to communicate with each other

Who can hear the language?

Who can speak with the language?

Is it the person who has pure soul?

Is it the person who knows a silent language?

The heavenly language may start from ear—spiritual ear

I am praying to learn how to listen to the mystery of silent language

To listen fully to sound in nature

To hear the Creator's reflection in his creating world

Stranger and Gypsy

What's the difference between stranger and gypsy?

Is a gypsy experiencing wind?

Or pretending ripeness?

How can I judge them?

Do they have an instinct about life as wind?

So much mystery

Who is this stranger?

Is he like a dandelion seed?

At the place of strangeness

Searching for the reason of his destiny

At the corner of the Deep South

Just seeding something meaningful?

But someday, I know, I must release everything

Even my dream, vision, and desire

Releasing is real wisdom and courage

What I want to possess is that knowledge

And then I will understand the mystery of unity with God

At the corner of the Deep South

Taste of Winter

The winter of Han River is reflecting on my mind

With a taste of grilled chestnut

With a taste of burned sweet potato

With a taste of icicle

With a taste of hunger

What are tastes of winter in Atlanta?

It may be;

With a taste of stranger

With a taste of dubious

With a taste of foolish

Insipid tastes

But a taste of spiritual

And a taste of existence

Some, Yes, Some

A like wind

A like cloud

A like rain

I stopped here

Nobody has an idea

Who will stop me?

Life is some journey

Some?

Yes, some

Universal some

Existential some

Divine some

Not the some, accidental

That is my confession of faith

Fathering

Never be an easy job

Fatherhood is the most blessed job in the world

but I don't know how I have been a father

It looks accidental

If I knew being a father was such a hard job

I wouldn't have been a father

or

I wouldn't have married my wife

I would prefer to be a bachelor boy, still

and then I would have traveled the globe

without any obligation to my children and wife

with many women, with uncountable dialogues

I would say with my ugly philosophy

And then

I would be stopped my life at the corner of the world

on the road that I never knew

Most meaningful and beautiful mission in the world

to have children

and to be a father

Even I am transforming to be a father, truly

I would love to say

Most blessed is to be a father and doing fathering

Theology and Me

Theology is a most attractive study

But almost it makes people arrogant

due to head knowledge

Do you know?

The distance from head to heart is so far

To achieve accordance between head and heart means to take your cross

Without self-denying with theology, nobody can attain the knowledge, truth

There was tremendous tragedy in the church

Childish persons who are theological technicians are also producing tremendously arrogant people

Such a bitter world

Dichotomous world

.

Contradictorily, I am also such a bitter man

with ignorance about theology

A Battle with Money

Is this destiny to battle with money in my life?

Most attractive temptation in my whole life

is money?

But I would like to speak out with my excuse

I am not such a low-dimension person

Struggle

Struggle

Struggle

Unavoidable reality

If I were a Father of Catholic Church

I would be free from money

due to no children

or wife

Divine vocational work with four children and wife—

is this a common struggle among Protestant clergymen?

Is this God's plan?

Due to understanding laypeople

Due to understanding reality

Why?

Because

spirituality is always reality

A Samaritan Woman

Nobody can avoid his or her reality

or circumstances

The mystery is, nobody can choose a birthplace

Nobody can choose a sex, man or woman

Nobody can choose wealth or poverty

Nobody can choose health or weakness

This kind of injustice is discussed within the Bible

as a human sight

How can we understand that kind of mystery?

Full of mysteries in the absolute truth

So, do we need His revelation?

Yes and yes

Interpretation with a reason in salvation

Knowing the truth,

relationship with God—

is that the way to truth?

Yes and yes

Audaciously, I like to say

when the Samaritan woman opened with her eyes,

she realized that she was in the relationship with Jesus as a real man
and husband

To meet a real man was impossible in the barren land of the
Samaritan woman

Even now man has a sinful nature

Just sweet water from a woman

and then a behavior likes to throw away a woman

That was such a long history and unceasing happening after Adam's
depravity

until the day of eschatology

The Proverbs Saying

Proverbs says,

"The poor man and the oppressor have this in common: The LORD gives light to the eyes of both."

Light to the eyes of both?

Yes, light.

Due to this light,

do human beings turn out to be equal?

There are tremendous ethnic backgrounds

There are tremendous cultures

There are tremendous characters

Uncountable characteristics, uniqueness, appearances …

So, can we say that we more than the whole world are?

The Bible says,

"For what shall it profit a man, if he shall gain the whole world, and lose his own soul?"

The value of soul is more than the whole world—

striking and powerful Word,

The principle of the kingdom of heaven!

Even a mustard seed, without light given from God,

is nothing.

But a trivial, small seed,

due to the light

has the potential to become a big tree.

Is that mystery of kingdom of heaven?

Like one mustard seed,

poor,

flawed like me

and naive to many,

but irresistible, thanks to my Lord,

due to His giving the light in my eyes.

This is a powerful blessing and wisdom,

the reason to live full of life.

A Coffee or a Cup of Coffee?

To a strange guy from Northeast Asia,

This language is usually confusing

A coffee or a cup of coffee?

Uncountable confusion in English

So, I use survival English in America

My daughter calls it "Broken English!"

Ashamed marching in America

But there is a way to living in this land

Tolerance,

Those patient American listeners

Most beautiful language is like tolerance

Is this language hidden in virtue?

Essentially, language is not verbal

Is that virtue?

Doggies

Doggies never betray their masters

Doggies never complain

Don't they know about complaining itself?

Anyhow, whenever I see you, I realize that you are sage

Best preacher

Best servant

Best obeying creature

If you were my friends

I would buy your wisdom

My Educating Is

I call my sons every day on the phone

Around 4:40 p.m.

Just after they have come home

Even I am an ugly father

I cannot stop calling them

To give a present

A habit

Reading habit, the Bible

My idea is to give them a lot of wisdom in the Bible, and then

To make them survive in this diverse and dynamic pluralistic world

I know this kind of calling would be stupidity, but

They may realize what father's love is when they reach their fifties, hopefully

Educating in this spoiled world and culture is difficult—a lot of spoiled kids

Explicit and split, two generations are those who know how to respect

Their parents and who don't know how to respect

Anyhow I will not give up that calling, even that

Is my selfish calling, stupid calling, or wise calling

I should be a militant father, at the some juncture of my life journey

And then I would leave my children to

My home

Catching Birds

Catching birds is an impossible mission

Some bird seeds in a cage

Even I have been waited for two weeks, but nothing happens at the cage. And then

It makes me ashamed, so next turn

Looks like a wrestle between cage and me

Folly wrestle

Ridiculous wrestle

Due to my self-respect

Some preacher saying, "Self-respect is sinful nature"

I am confirming my nature mingled with my sin

Old Books in My Basement

I am sorry, sorry, and sorry,

ignoring a lot of authors who lived in the 1800s and early 1900s—

just put them in my basement, like a jail, and then

I never open and read those books.

There are tremendous chances to meet those old authors

but I usually have ignored them, so I feel guilty.

How can I send my apology to them?

The way to meet those old, respectful authors is to read, and then I would like to

say, "Sorry, sir! I will learn your wisdom, knowledge, theology, and so on."

I will do, and do,

because I am listening to their voices in the basement, when I

sleep and leave my home.

Forgotten treasures, undiscovered treasures, and hidden authors—

I am tyranny.

Who Are Southerners?

I heard the Southerners are rednecks.

It might be bias.

Redneck?

I never knew this word.

When I visited Helen, Georgia, there was a picture captioned "redneck"—

a picture of men catching fish and deer with TNT.

What a biased image!

My experiences with Southerners haven't brought those images.

Sin is to create a bad image by painting someone's background,

like propaganda,

the method of communists.

Uncountable people like to use that paintbrush, and then

plant some prejudicial ideas.

Is this the history of civilization? And

also is this a personal history?

Unceasing battle.

When I Saw My Son's Football Game

When I saw my son's football game at the town playground,

I felt I was a successful immigrant person:

a moment of pride, and

a feeling of compensation, and

an answer to the question, "Why did I come to America?"—

a tearful moment.

If my children pay back that American grace with their excellent leadership,

my mission will be almost done, and

if my children can live for His kingdom,

my destiny will be successful.

Saying Hello!

Pretending moment

saying hello!

Selfish moment

saying hello!

Cultural difference and

shallow, external appearances

saying hello!

It's almost a taste like plain city water

The guy from the third world couldn't understand that kind of greeting

Avoiding freezing atmosphere between guys

saying hello!

A moment of breaking ice

A great tool in the world

Now, I am enjoying

saying hello!

Let It Be Me

A famous song is "Let It Be Me"

Is this a song of naturalism?

I don't know what the background is, but

The image closes up about nature

Nature, I would like to say, the meaning of mine, "itself and will be" by Chinese character,

May be …

The meaning of the word "nature" is profound to understand

The Western side may explain it more physically, and the Eastern side

More philosophically

Anyhow, who can understand this huge word "nature"?

"Let it be me" is a sentence like "wind"

A contradictory but charming word,

Invincible word, abstract word, and idealistic word

"Let it be me"

It looks egoistic and spoiled

But it demands balancing in man's life

The essential hope of human beings: "Let it be me"

This phrase is a kind of mature scale of man

So, I feel still a child

Everlasting child

The Café Vincent

Usually I visit the Café Vincent

whenever I need to write my book—

such a convenient place for writing, resting, listening, imaging, sharing, and catharsis.

It's such an asylum for those immigrant people, usually Koreans.

When people come to this asylum,

strangely they become cheerful and bright,

because they can speak in their mother language,

and they can share the common culture and emotions.

The café is the only place to have the illusion of being somewhere in South Korea:

Anyang, Seongnam, Gangnam, Seocho, Incheon, and so on.

Common feelings they are expressing; homesickness, or missing friends, mothers, siblings, fathers, old lovers ...

... hometown memories, and so on ....

But the paradox is

privileged people who know what the losing is, the meaning of homesick,

mother language, and transition from the one generation to the next generation.

Time Is So Fast

Usually people say, "Time is so fast"

Especially about the time of America

I don't know what the real reason is

I also confess my experiencing with time

With same feeling in America

Without period (.), just flowing like the wind

In the city of *Gone with the Wind*

Time is such a girl I couldn't grasp at, the time past young days

So, God has lessoned his people through the first love, mystery love

That is unattained truth, and a hidden mystery

Time always demands that people interpret tremendous hidden meanings through times

But time is no guarantee of the maturity to interpret those hidden meanings

To fast, to be matured

Time is such a critical being, to know who I was, and I am

Just going by divine time

Without chance to know me, and experiences with me

Resisting and resisting what the meaning of my life is, to time

But will I be one of those people who don't know who they are?

Just aging, with my face with withering

Under the fast time

Same routine with others

Is the time such a ruthlessness?

Is that a kind of physical thing?

Or

A faithful servant of Lord

Like those servants in Ezekiel?

"They turned not when they went; they went every one straight forward"

Nobody can hold the time

That is universal truth

No period

But some juncture of divine time, there will be a period

So, time is such a fast to fulfill His will.

Without and with considering our time

Time is so fast.

Inerasable Memories to a Man

There are several memories inerasable to a man

Those are usually the memories of being beaten by some guys

Without any falsehood of mine,

Without any reason,

When some guy was using his stick or military shovel to beat me,

I couldn't understand,

But after prayer, it turned to such a good memory

Tremendous happenings in the man's world were a good memory

In the young days, in the man's society with same uniform

Strangely, no scars, even after a lot of being beaten

Due to different province

Due to other buddies' mistakes

Due to uncomfortable feeling of seniors

Due to no hard liquor, to seniors

Impossible business with seniors who were from all over the provinces

Almost every midnight there were some happenings, up until dawn

Strangely these things made a great soldier's spirit

That was the mystery of men's life

We had called the period of military service "Life University"

Strange university

The degree was a sergeant

What a great degree—better than any doctoral degree!

When I Raised My Children

It was a critical time

when I raised up my children

No chance to be a father and fathering

Usually back and forth,

to seminary,

to library,

to church,

to home

I may feel apologetic to my children until I pass away

without caring well for them as a father

But with caring by God's hand

they have been raised up until now

That is a great touching of my Lord

Still now, He is caring my daughters and sons

He is always the Father on behalf of me

Thanks, Lord!

A Most Pleasant Moment

A most pleasant moment is after church members have gone on Sunday

A time to be alone

With a moment of prayer to reflect on my sermon and

Recall members, face by face

And then something wrong, when I find

I feel some kind of depression

Is this a common mind-set of ministers?

When I was ordained, a moderator from the presbytery preached from Proverbs,

"Be sure you know the condition of your flocks, give careful attention to your herds"

Even though these words have been scribed on my heart, I can feel guilt as a pastor

So, this chance of the most pleasant moment turns to be unpleasant

A time being for me a pleasant time, selfish time

A time being for reflecting on my members, a time to know the Lord's heart

Paradoxical time

Shameful and depressing, and then challenging to my preaching and laziness

How many such hiding places in my ministry are there?

A ministering job fills up with sin faster than any other job in the world

A Time to Cry

When I see a river, clouds, rain, and swaying trees,

I cry

When I see His wisdom in my trivial, ordinary times,

I cry

When I see His breathing in my walking in the folly way,
.
.
.

I cry

After I Have Sinned

A time to give up everything, that's a time to have sinned,

Money, honor, possessions, fame, popularity, recognition, seductive things,

Love, a temptation to be the winner, a deep internal anger, spring of bitter water in nature,

Irresistible hating from nature, and so on, and on, endless

The voyage of life is like traveling across the field of sinful mines

How many times have I died?

Death with holy things, and

Resurrection with sin

Today was dead day

Just in my home, I wondered around

Nowhere to go,

I know, pretending with a smile, and acting like a righteous person

To people

And being called, Christian and minister

It's heavy, like a mountain

So I have tried and tried to escape the weight of my soul

With prayer and pleading to my Lord

Still I feel my dark soul

Disappointed with myself

Is life like this kind of circulation?

Wrestling between cross and accusation of nature

To See Is to Believe?

To see is to believe

That I have learned when I was a student

Time has been passed

as I have gotten old

The meaning has been changed

…..

There are dark worlds

due to my sin

So,

I have learned

to see is not to believe,

because I have seen a lot of dirty worlds

due to my sin

It means that my eyes has been opened

and I have been seeing I was naked

My nature has tried to hide my sin with my apron—

the temporary apron

So, to see is to cover

At the Rainy Day

The rainy day is a seductive day

To drink a coffee at the café, Mozart

To walk along the way of Mars Hill

To write unfinished poems

To cry with the sad novel, "a dialogue with love and soul"

To search my young days at the station of Cheongnyangri, Seoul

To ride the train's KyungChun line with my wife, back to twenty-three years ago

To recover my lost love

And,

To visit the village I was born

Guilty Feeling

"And the eyes of them both were opened, and they knew that they were naked"

Is this a universal thing—our eyes being opened after falling to sin?

It takes a very critical reading of the Word to understand it.

Usually after falling to sin, people experience a broken relationship

between God and man

due to man's guilty feeling.

The guilty feeling always requires some hiding place.

So, we have a dream at the night

to liberate our oppression by guilty feeling.

Daytime means jail, but nighttime means freedom

due to dreaming

that is a great gift from a loving God

for ordinary people.

But how can we erase our scars from guilt?

Dreaming is only a temporary asylum,

because there are no more dreams after death—

is that reality?

Punishment of sin after death,

natural knowledge from our nature—

is that human bondage?

A clue:

"And ye shall know the truth, and the truth shall make you free."

Epilogue

I feel some guilt at having written these poems.

As a person who doesn't use English as a first language, I have tried to communicate my inner voices and some dynamics through the poems, but I feel that I am an abuser of English.

So I offer my apologies to my respecting readers.

I struggle with English, especially grammar. The grammar is more law than gospel to those people who don't know English. So it makes people lose a taste for my language, or even find my speech audacious. Maybe if I knew English grammar well, I would overcome those obstacles.

I learned English when I was a middle-school boy. Usually, language teachers taught students with a stick in those days. When the teacher pushed students to memorize a tremendous number of words, students became tense and avoided English, as it was a stressful burden. Despite how stressful the lessons were, my teacher taught English grammar without providing any overall context. So whenever I think of learning English, I think of a difficult and burdensome study that I had to undertake, because the dominant language in the world is English. English is a gateway to promotion and success, so tremendous numbers of people from the third world have to learn English, and then they lose their mother language. So to learn English means to lose their mother language. Earning and losing—that is the language battle. This kind of battle will never cease until the end of world.

What is the meaning of English to those people from the third world? Is it a tool of business, survival, and stress? Can it be a tool of being? Those people who don't speak English fluently are burdened, even if they speak some language.

Is this the Babel effect? In the Bible, this effect started from human sin, so language can mean some burdens and struggles. Language also offers a way to understand humanity. For this reason, people may like to express their inner struggle and spiritual thirst by using the human tool of language and heavenly metaphor.

Thanks!

Young Jun Kim

ABOUT THE AUTHOR

Young Jun Kim was born in Seoul Korea in 1958, the after five years of truce in Korean War. His experience of childhood was so poor as the other Korean at those times and this experience became the author's background colors to understand humanity.

Those school days of author's elementary, middle and high were tremendous memories, unique experience, and he was just a simple and normal student. However his experience at the Korean Army was a great opportunity to understand about reality and diversity to form his world view. Those stories may be published in a future.

When he was a college student, he studied the major on architecture. But his hinge point to be a minister was from his Divine calling at his junior days. Even he knows his way to go, due to Divine calling, he studied more at a graduate school with a major urban design.

When the author felt to study more in America, he came to small town of Deep South, Erskine Theological Seminary, which located in Due West of South Carolina.

In this school, he learned a lot of treasured things like the relationship with professors and friends, tradition, pietism, southern culture a little and theology. At the last, the author finished his degrees with M. div, MATS, MACE, and Doctor of Ministry.

Now, the author involves several vocational works; teaching as an associate professor at Georgia Christian University, ministering as a senior pastor at Atlanta Saints Presbyterian Church, a columnist of Korean South East News and Atlanta daily News, and a hospice chaplain at MeSun.

Even the author feels a shame to do such a many vocational works to compare his ability, but the author often says God wants to his profit from him, due to God's investment to him.

This book is an expression of lost mind as a stranger, spiritual thirsty, and eschatological hope. When the author tries to write a poetry book, it made the author feel guilty, because he didn't much know about language, especially English. So he would like to say himself as a folly and naïve stranger.

The author wrote two Korean books, An Essayistic Spiritual Journal of a naïve Stranger (2008) and Overlook with Church (2007).

People call him as a rich man, because he has four children (Lee-Lye, EeSl, Isaac, Isaiah) and his lovingly wife Mee Sook Kim. And now the author remains walking in His foot prints.